Learn about... TEXAS DINOSAURS

A Learning and Activity Book

Color your own field guide to the dinosaurs that once roamed Texas

Designed and Illustrated by

Elena T. Ivy

Concept and Text by

Georg Zappler

Consulting Editor

Juliann Pool

PWD BK P4504-094-N 8/94

Another "Learn about Texas" publication from

TEXAS PARKS AND WILDLIFE PRESS

ISBN:0-9636765-7-1

In this **Learn about Texas Dinosaurs** book, you will meet all the prehistoric animals called dinosaurs that have been found on Texas soil.

Please remember that dinosaurs are a special group of reptiles that inhabited our planet from 225 to 65 million years ago. And, that means that dinosaurs lived and died out long, long before there were any humans. Dinosaurs lived only on land; they did not fly or swim. Some dinosaurs, however, are thought to be the ancestors of birds.

These are dinosaurs:

a ***Alamosaurus***

b ***Tyrannosaurus***

c ***Coelophysis***

d ***Ornithomimus***

e ***Kritosaurus***

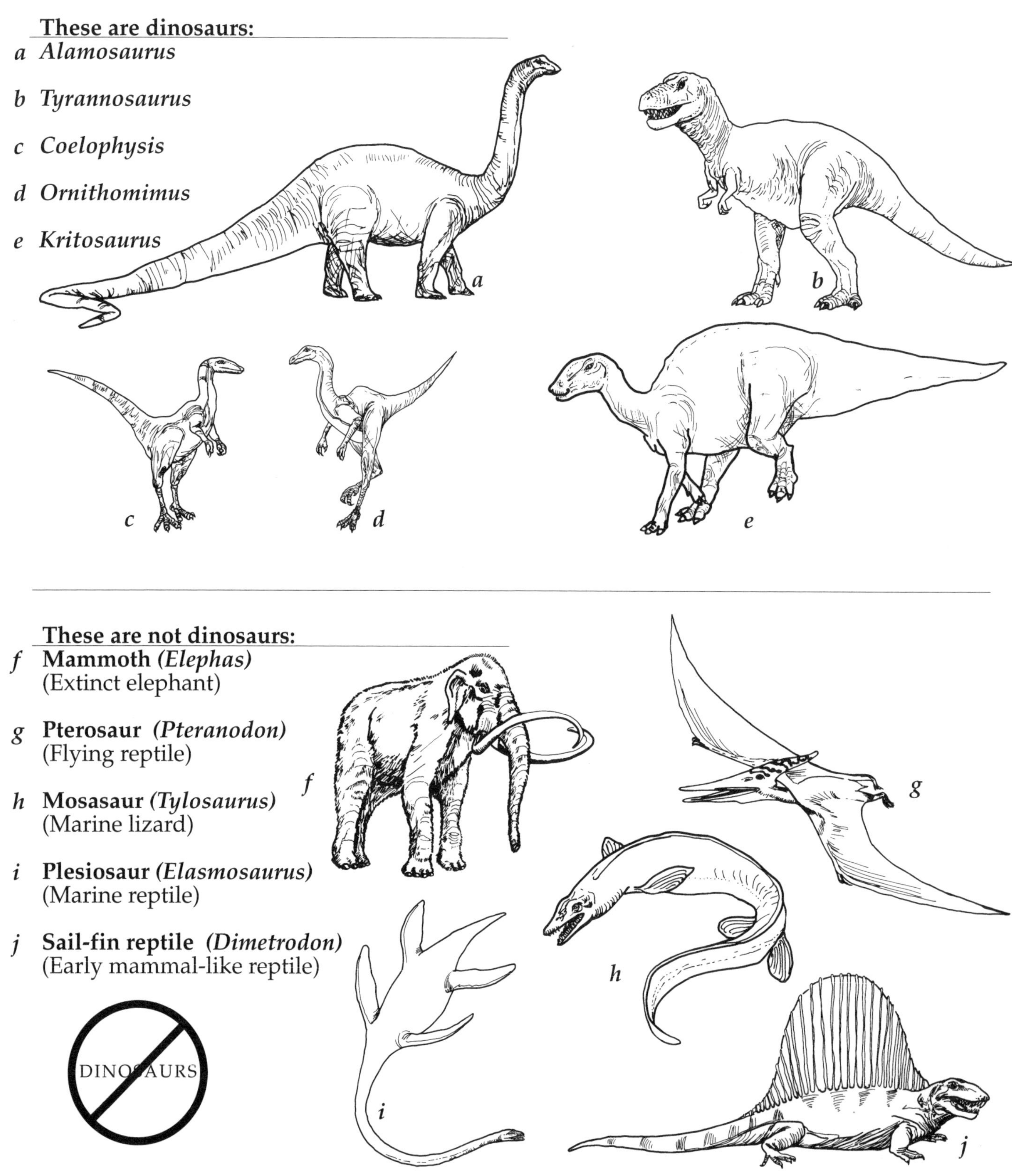

These are not dinosaurs:

f **Mammoth *(Elephas)***
(Extinct elephant)

g **Pterosaur *(Pteranodon)***
(Flying reptile)

h **Mosasaur *(Tylosaurus)***
(Marine lizard)

i **Plesiosaur *(Elasmosaurus)***
(Marine reptile)

j **Sail-fin reptile *(Dimetrodon)***
(Early mammal-like reptile)

Texas Dinosaur Finds

Many different sorts of fossils are found in Texas. Among these fossils are the preserved bones and tracks of dinosaurs.

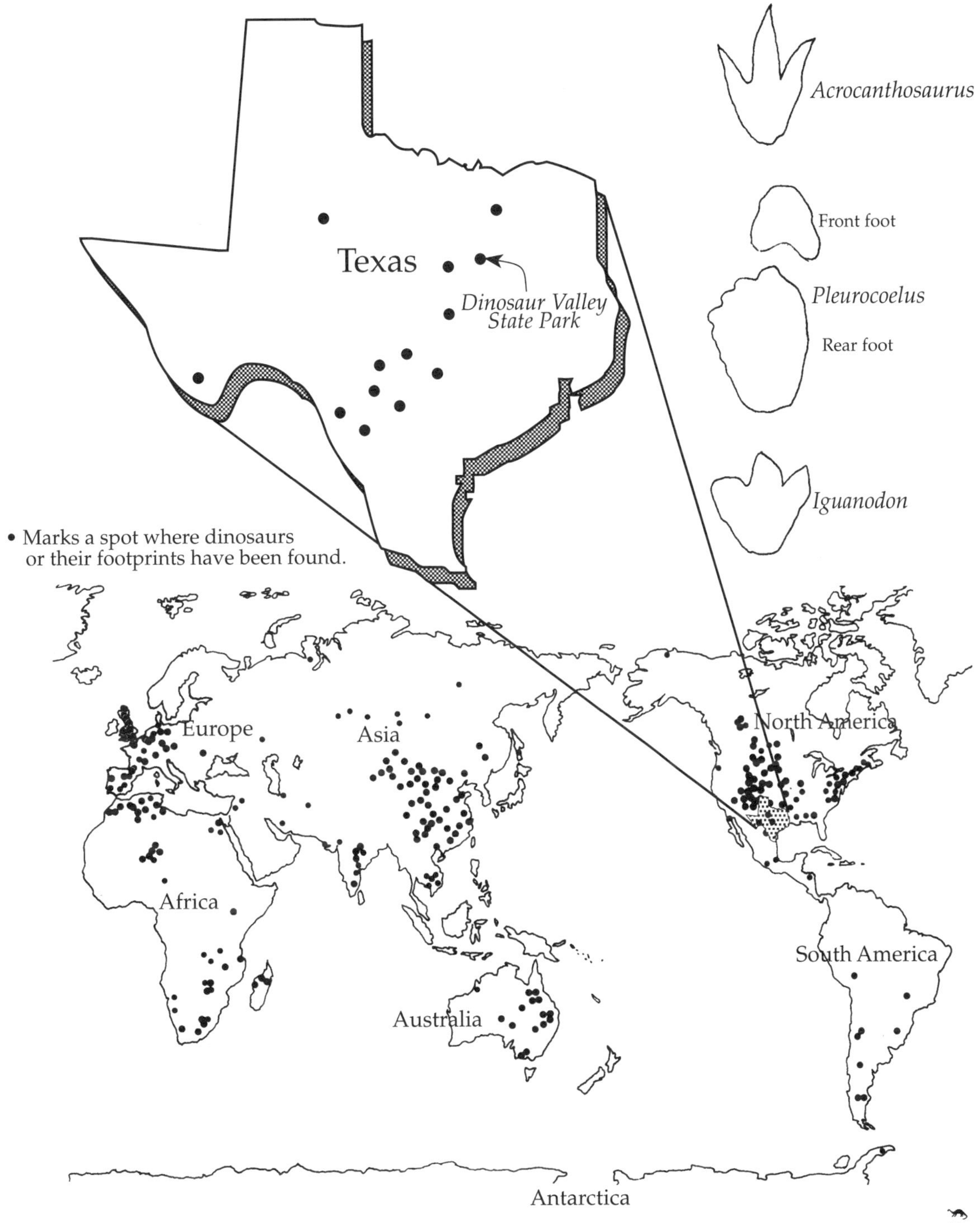

Texas

Dinosaur Valley State Park

Acrocanthosaurus

Front foot

Pleurocoelus

Rear foot

Iguanodon

• Marks a spot where dinosaurs or their footprints have been found.

Europe

Asia

North America

Africa

South America

Australia

Antarctica

Texas has 17 of the about 300 kinds of dinosaurs known worldwide.

A **kind** of dinosaur means what biologists call a **genus**. Each genus is made up of one or more **species**. Thus, for example, *Tyrannosaurus* is a genus and *Tyrannosaurus rex* is one of the species of that genus.

Most **genera** (plural of genus) of dinosaurs have only one species. When talking about dinosaurs and other extinct animals only the genus name is commonly used.

17 dinosaurs

300 dinosaurs

Geology of Texas

Texas's dinosaurs—like all dinosaurs—lived during the Mesozoic Era of geological time, from 248 to 65 million years ago. This geological division, in turn, is made up of three periods:

1) the Triassic Period, lasting from 248 to 208 million years ago
2) the Jurassic Period, lasting from 208 to 144 million years ago and
3) the Cretaceous Period, lasting from 144 to 65 million years ago.

Texas's Triassic rock deposits are all from what are called **Late Triassic** times, 225 to 220 million years ago. The first or earliest "batch" of Texas dinosaurs comes from such rocks found east of Lubbock in the Panhandle region of Texas.

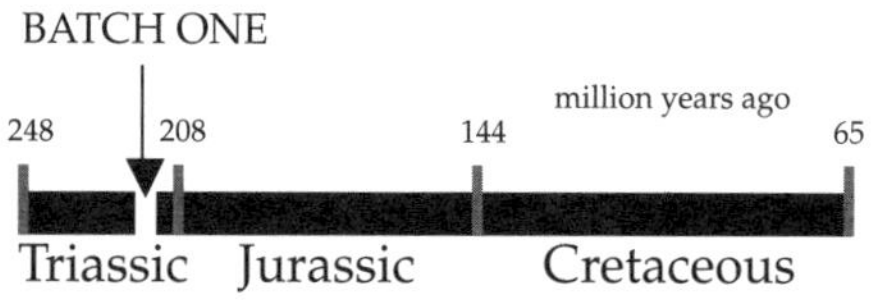

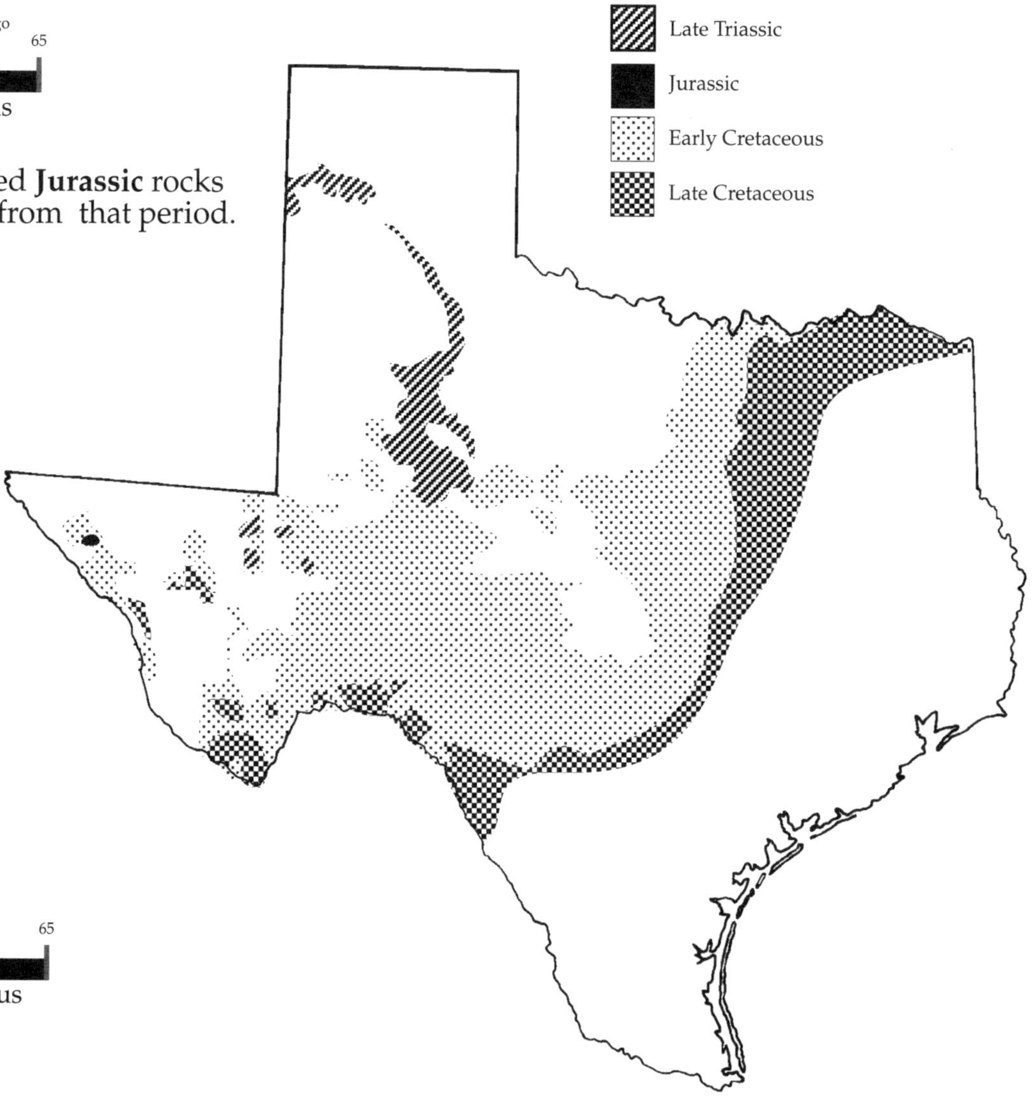

BATCH ONE
million years ago
248 208 144 65
Triassic Jurassic Cretaceous

Late Triassic
Jurassic
Early Cretaceous
Late Cretaceous

Texas has hardly any exposed **Jurassic** rocks and therefore no dinosaurs from that period.

Texas has lots of Cretaceous rock deposits. Some of those, from what are called **Early Cretaceous** times, are found exposed on the surface in a broad belt that runs through central Texas. The second "batch" of Texas dinosaurs is found in such rocks, from about 110 to 105 million years ago. Dinosaur tracks and fossil bones are found at many different locations within this belt of rocks.

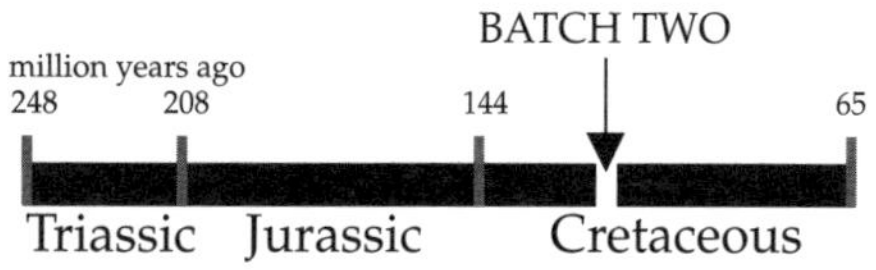

BATCH TWO
million years ago
248 208 144 65
Triassic Jurassic Cretaceous

The third "batch" of Texas dinosaurs comes from **Late Cretaceous** rocks. Such rocks lie exposed on the surface in a belt next to the Early Cretaceous rocks and also in several areas in West Texas. So far, dinosaurs have been found only in the Big Bend region of West Texas, in rocks that are 75 to 65 million years old.

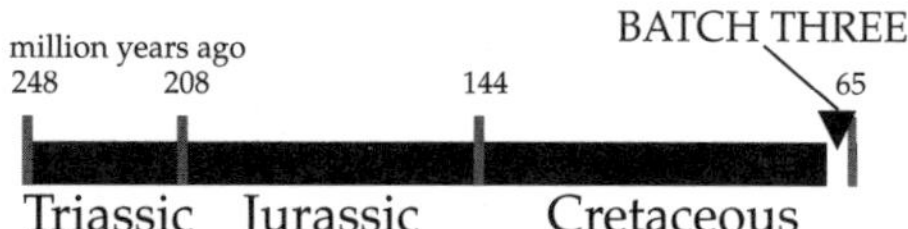

How Dinosaurs are Classified

How do paleontologists (the scientists who study fossils) decide that a fossil skeleton they find belongs to a dinosaur and not a lizard or crocodile or some other kind of reptile?

Well, when it comes to classifying dinosaurs, it's the structure of the pelvis—or the hip bones—that counts.

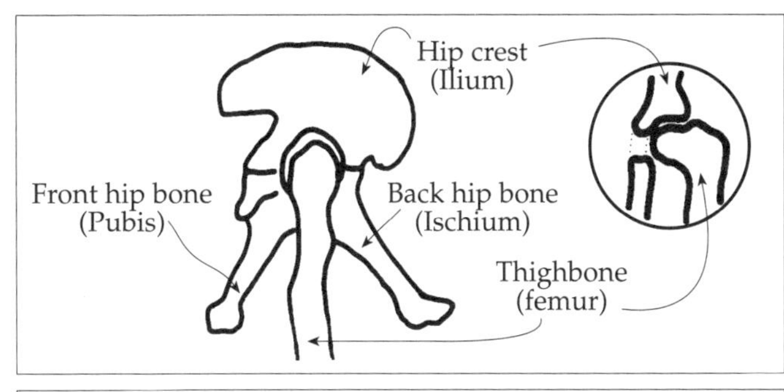

To begin with, among reptiles, only dinosaurs have a hole where the three bones that form each side of the pelvis come together. This hole is a socket for holding the inturned head typical of the dinosaur thighbone or femur.

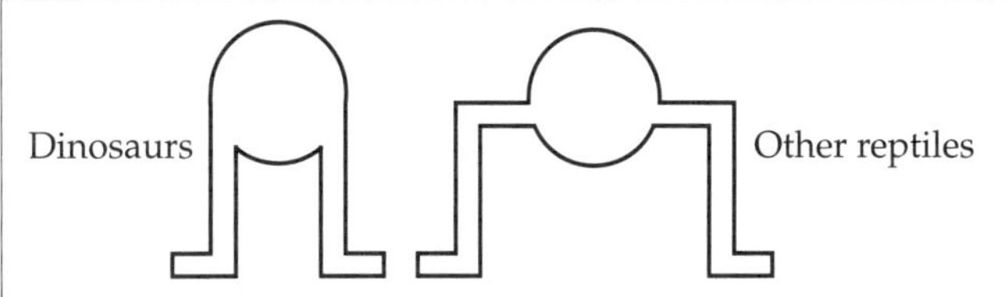

That way, dinosaurs could swing their legs close to the body, giving them an erect gait like horses and dogs and other mammals. Reptiles other than dinosaurs have sprawled-out limbs as they walk with their belly close to the ground.

Secondly, dinosaurs are divided into two main groups depending on how the three hip bones on each side are joined together.

In the group called **Lizard-hips** (or Saurischia), the two lower hip bones point away from each other. (This is similar to what we see in lizards and other living reptiles).

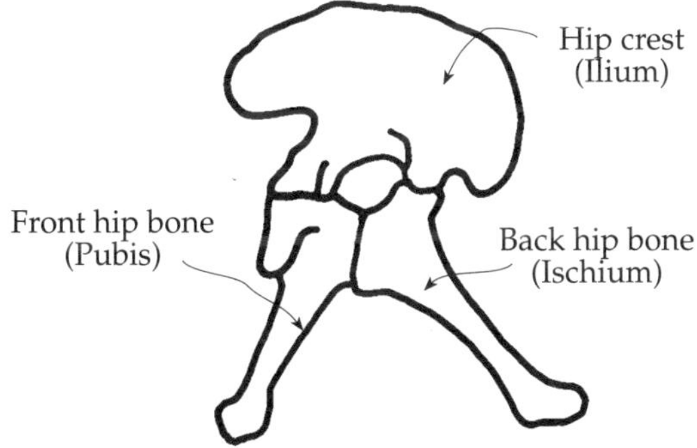

In the group called **Bird-hips** (or Ornithischia), the two lower hip bones both point towards the rear. (This is similar to what we see in birds. Please remember, however, that the dinosaurs most closely related to birds are the lizard-hips and not the bird-hips).

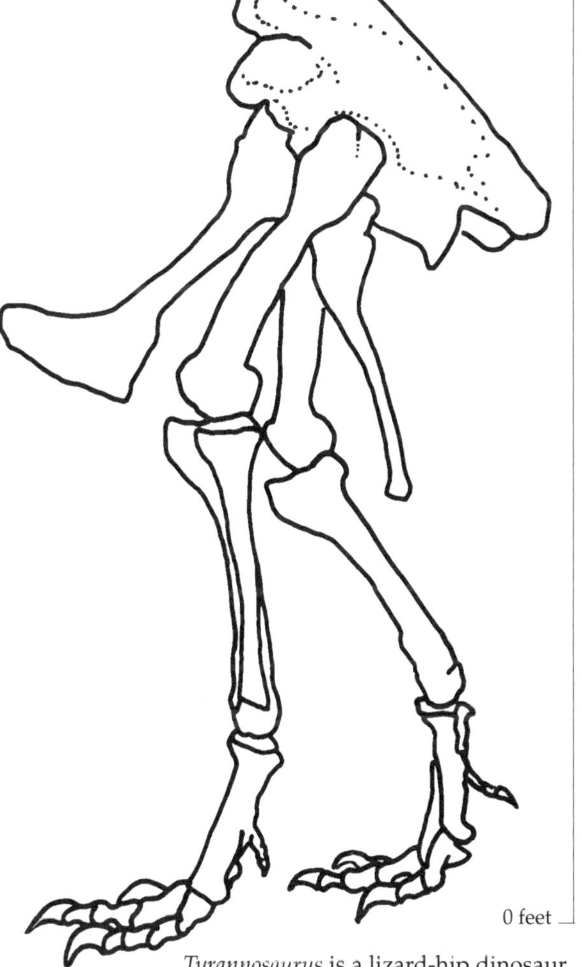

Tyrannosaurus is a lizard-hip dinosaur.

BATCH ONE

The oldest (earliest) "batch" of Texas dinosaurs lived from about 225 to 220 million years ago. Fossils of dinosaurs of that time are found in Late Triassic rocks located in the Panhandle region of Texas. During those days much of that area was part of a tropical inland basin surrounded on all sides by mountains. Tall (from-100-to-200-foot-high) pine-like evergreen trees and cycads (trees with stubby trunks and palm-like leaves) grew on well-drained soils. In the swampy lowlands, criss-crossed by streams and dotted with numerous ponds, grew ferns and horsetails (scouring rushes).

Water-dwelling backboned animals included numerous primitive fishes, strange 10-foot-long flat-bodied amphibians called metoposaurs and crocodile-like reptiles called phytosaurs. Among the animals sharing the land with the dinosaurs was a fierce 20-foot-long, two-legged meat-eating reptile called *Postosuchus*, several kinds of plant-eating reptiles called aetosaurs, and what may be the first known bird, called *Protoavis*.

TECHNOSAURUS

TECK-noh-SORE-us

Technosaurus FACT BOX

Length: 4 feet
Weight: 25 pounds
Time: 225 - 220 million years ago
Where Found: Texas
Classification: Early two-legged bird-hip.
Notable Notes: One of the very first bird-hips. Similar small plant-eating dinosaurs are known from South Africa.

million years ago
248 208 144 65
Triassic Jurassic Cretaceous

Technosaurus means "techno lizard" because it was found near Texas Tech University. This dinosaur was no longer that a large dog. It had ridged teeth for cutting up the plants it ate. It browsed on all-fours, but ran on its hind legs. The main enemies were the meat-eating dinosaur *Coelophysis* and the large reptile *Postosuchus*.

COELOPHYSIS

SEEL-oh-FIE-sis

Coelophysis FACT BOX

Length: 10 feet
Weight: 60 pounds
Time: 225 - 220 million years ago
Where Found: New Mexico, Arizona, Texas
Classification: A coelurosaur or small meat-eating lizard-hip.
Notable Notes: One of the very first meat-eating lizard-hips. Well known from hundreds of skeletons found buried in New Mexico.

million years ago
248 208 144 65
Triassic Jurassic Cretaceous

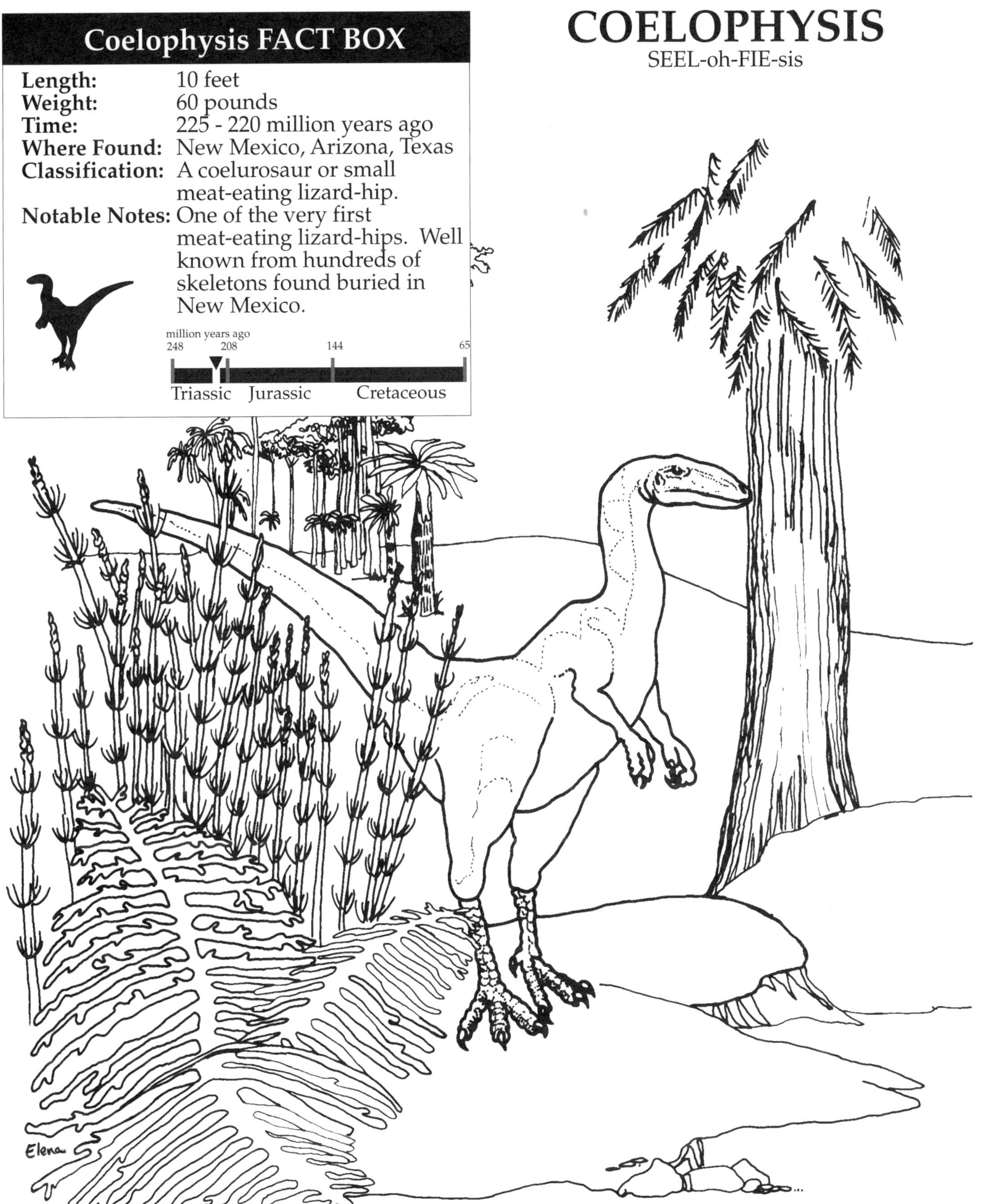

Coelophysis means "hollow form" because of its hollow bones. This dinosaur was a small, fast-moving, two-legged, sharp-toothed hunter. It moved in large packs, capturing early lizards, tiny mammal-like reptiles and small plant-eating dinosaurs like *Technosaurus*. Its main enemy was the large aggressive reptile *Postosuchus*.

SHUVOSAURUS

SHOO-voh-SORE-us

Shuvosaurus FACT BOX

Length:	10 feet
Weight:	250 pounds
Time:	225 - 220 million years ago
Where Found:	Texas
Classification:	An ornithomimid or "ostrich" lizard-hip.
Notable Notes:	The earliest known ostrich dinosaur. Only the skull was found.

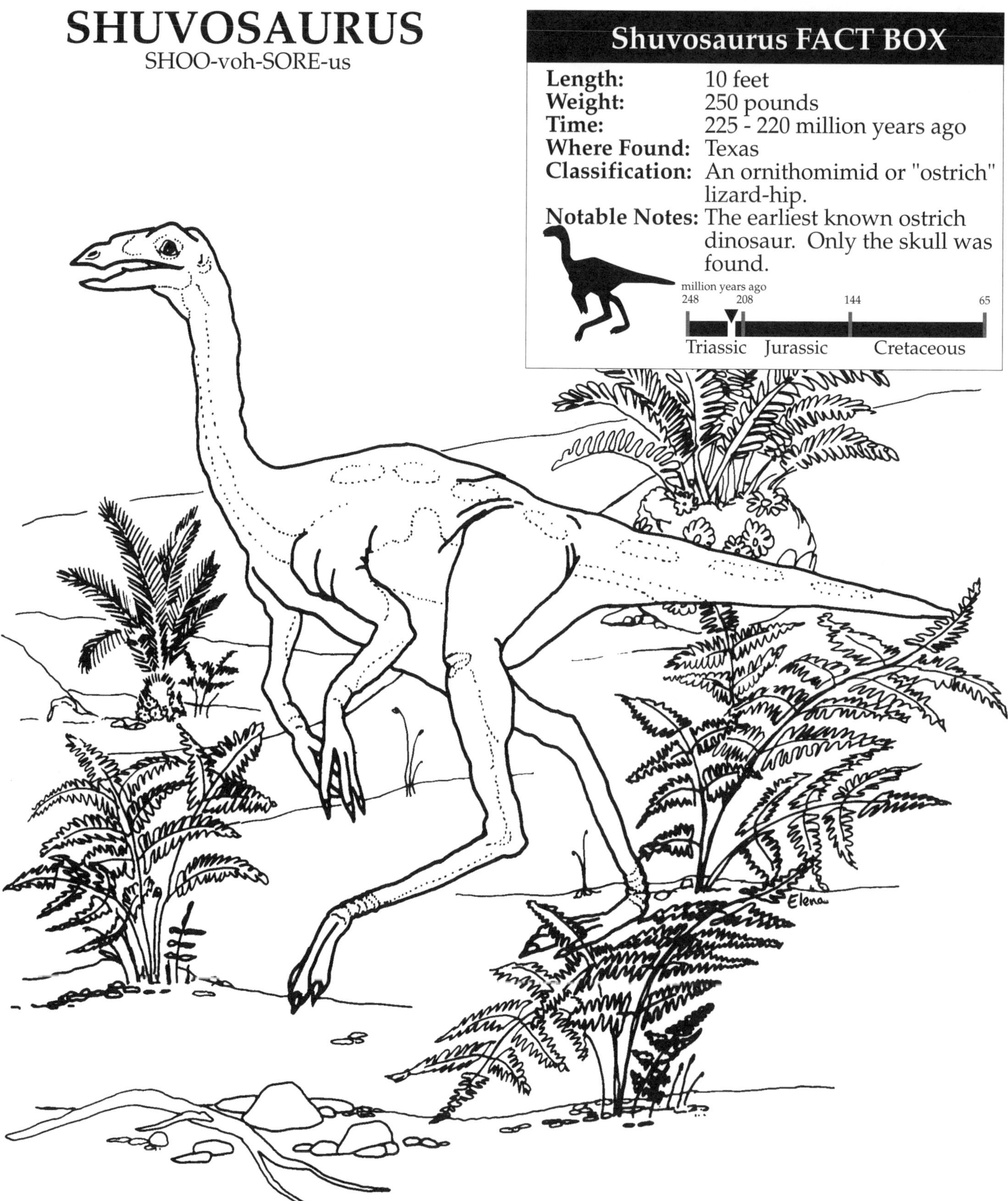

Shuvosaurus means "Shuvo's lizard" after the name of the son of the paleontologist who discovered this dinosaur. It looked like a big ostrich, except that it didn't have feathers. This dinosaur had a short heavy beak that covered toothless jaws. The beak was shaped to crack hard-shelled nuts and seeds efficiently. However, *Shuvosarus* probably ate other plant materials as well, along with any small animals it could catch.

Word Search Game

Find the words in the puzzle. They may be backwards, diagonal, across, up or down.

Words																	
ACROCANTHOSAURUS	A	C	R	O	C	A	N	T	H	O	S	A	U	R	U	S	P
ALAMOSAURUS	A	R	E	A	D	I	N	G	K	A	I	N	D	O	U	F	R
ARCHEOLOGY	T	E	E	D	I	N	O	T	U	R	T	L	E	L	S	A	E
ARMOR-PLATED	Y	T	U	R	M	E	A	R	N	S	T	H	T	E	E	T	H
BEDROCK	R	A	E	S	G	F	O	S	S	I	L	A	C	I	E	N	I
BONE	A	C	T	I	E	P	F	I	C	C	O	A	T	E	G	O	S
CARNIVORE	N	E	R	Y	O	O	F	G	E	C	I	S	S	A	I	R	T
CLAY	N	O	E	D	L	N	U	S	L	I	Z	A	R	D	S	S	O
COLD-BLOODED	O	U	E	N	O	B	C	A	R	N	I	V	O	R	E	U	R
CRETACEOUS	S	S	C	H	G	A	Z	S	T	Y	R	A	D	N	N	O	I
DINOSAURS	A	S	A	U	Y	T	R	S	U	S	A	E	E	A	C	H	C
ERA	U	Y	A	R	E	N	E	G	C	R	D	O	N	T	A	S	I
FORMATION	R	G	N	U	S	O	N	E	M	O	O	R	M	O	C	U	R
FOSSIL	U	O	Q	E	R	E	L	O	O	A	T	E	D	I	S	L	P
GENERA	S	L	E	C	I	E	R	L	S	T	Y	R	S	A	N	E	Y
GEOLOGY	N	O	O	S	A	P	B	U	R	U	S	S	R	E	X	O	G
JURASSIC	F	T	O	E	L	D	I	N	O	S	A	U	R	S	E	C	O
LIMESTONE	X	N	A	A	L	I	M	P	L	R	E	I	S	O	N	O	L
LIZARDS	E	O	T	O	O	N	F	S	U	E	V	E	R	A	L	R	O
PALEONTOLOGY	S	E	C	P	E	O	C	J	B	E	D	R	O	C	K	U	E
PLEUROCOELUS	D	L	I	E	S	S	O	L	I	M	E	S	T	O	N	E	H
PREHISTORIC	F	A	T	H	E	A	G	E	N	U	S	T	Y	Y	A	L	C
QUETZALCOATLUS	R	P	A	N	N	U	N	O	I	T	A	M	R	O	F	P	R
READING	T	E	X	A	S	R	S	U	R	U	A	S	O	M	A	L	A
SAUROPOD	M	A	N	Y	D	I	F	F	E	R	E	N	T	S	O	R	T
TEETH	S	O	F	F	O	S	S	I	L	S	A	R	E	F	O	U	N
TEXAS	D	I	N	T	E	X	A	S	A	M	O	N	G	T	H	E	S
TRIASSIC	E	F	O	S	S	I	L	S	A	R	E	T	H	E	P	R	E
TURTLE	S	E	R	V	E	D	B	O	N	E	S	A	N	D	T	R	A
TYRANNOSAURUS	C	K	S	O	F	D	I	N	O	S	A	U	R	S	E	A	T

BATCH TWO

1 *Pleurocoelus*
2 *Acrocanthosaurus*
3 *Iguanodon*
4 *Naomichelys*
5 *Goniopholis*
6 pterosaur
7 cycad
8 fern
9 horsetail

The second oldest "batch" of Texas dinosaurs lived from about 110 to 105 million years ago. Fossils of dinosaurs and their footprints of that time are found in Early Cretaceous rocks located throughout north-central and central Texas. The dinosaurs left their footprints and sometimes their skeletons, in marshy tidal flats bordering what was then the Gulf of Mexico. Inland from the muddy shores were forests of cone-bearing trees and cycads. Sharing this environment with the dinosaurs were crocodiles, turtles and flying reptiles.

The attack scene above is based on two actual fossil dinosaur trackways. These preserved tracks show an *Acrocanthosaurus* following and lunging at a *Pleurocoelus.*

DEINONYCHUS

die-NON-i-kus

Deinonychus FACT BOX

Length: 10 feet
Weight: 150 pounds
Time: 110 - 105 million years ago
Where Found: Montana, Wyoming, Texas
Classification: A theropod or meat-eating lizard-hip.
Notable Notes: The second toe on each hind foot carried a 5 inch-long, movable, sickle-shaped claw capable of ripping apart much larger prey.

million years ago
248 208 144 65
Triassic Jurassic Cretaceous

Deinonychus means "terrible claw" because of the sickle-shaped hind-foot claw. This dinosaur probably hunted in packs, attacking much larger plant-eating dinosaurs like *Tenontosaurus*. In addition to its fearsome sickle claws, *Deinonychus* had dagger-like saw-edged teeth and powerful front limbs armed with sharp claws.

ACROCANTHOSAURUS

a-kroh-kan-thoh-SORE-us

Acrocanthosaurus FACT BOX

Length: 30 feet
Weight: 3 tons
Time: 110 - 105 million years ago
Where Found: Texas, Oklahoma
Classification: A carnosaur, or large meat-eating lizard-hip.
Notable Notes: A series of footprints at Dinosaur Valley State Park in Glen Rose, Texas show this dinosaur chasing and attacking *Pleurocoelus*.

million years ago
248 208 144 65
Triassic Jurassic Cretaceous

Acrocanthosaurus means "top-spined lizard" from the ridge of spines along its back. This dinosaur left hundreds of three-toed fossil footprints throughout central and north-central Texas. Nobody knows the function of the muscular ridge along its back. Its pointed teeth were serrated along the edges like steak knives.

PLEUROCOELUS

PLEW-roh-SEEL-us

Pleurocoelus FACT BOX

Length: 45 feet
Weight: 10 tons
Time: 110 - 105 million years ago
Where Found: Texas, Maryland, England
Classification: A sauropod or giant four-legged plant-eating lizard-hip.
Notable Notes: Traveled in groups with the young on the inside, so they could be protected by the larger adults.

million years ago
248 208 144 65
Triassic Jurassic Cretaceous

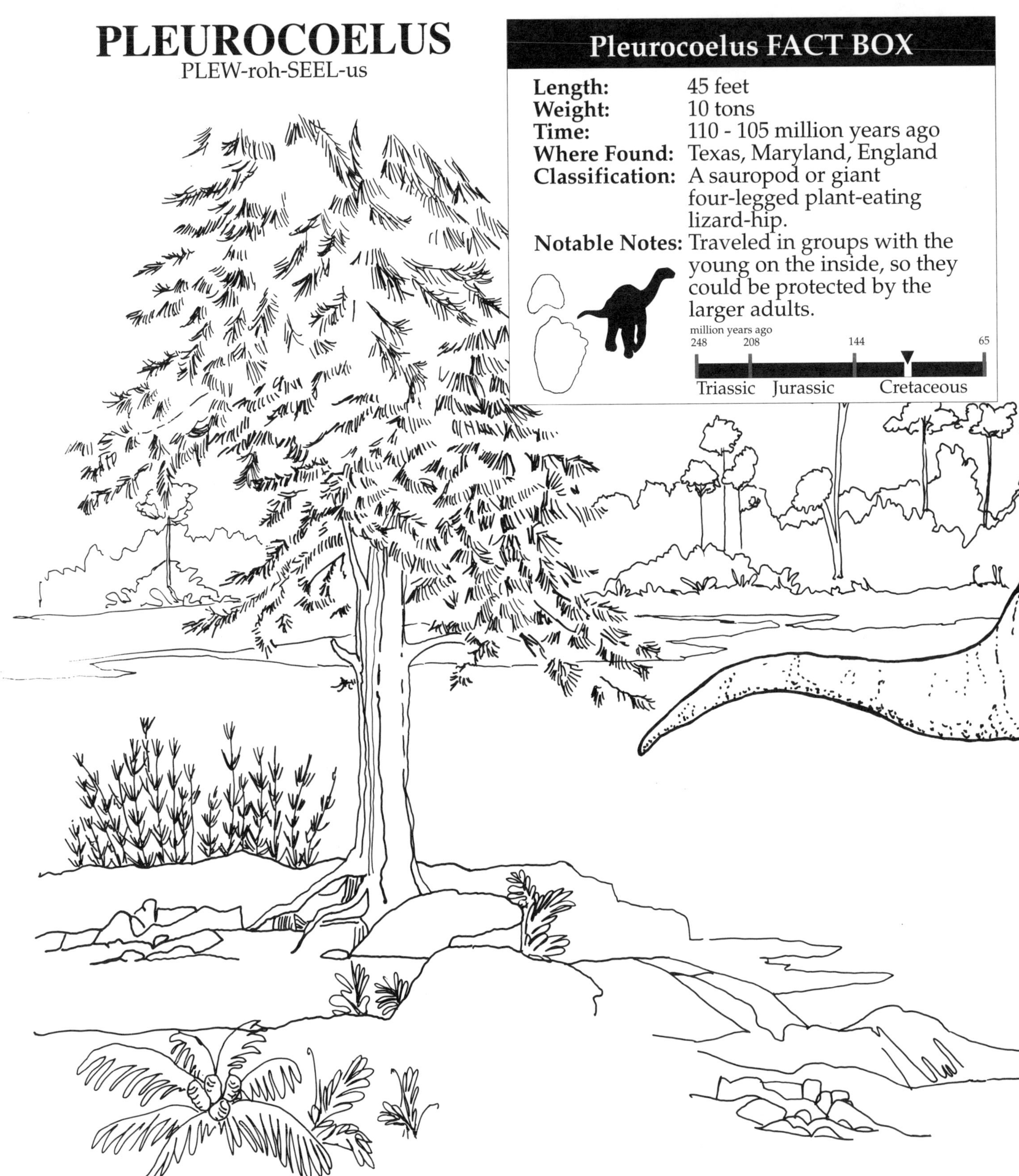

Pleurocoelus means "hollow side" because of the way its vertebrae are scooped out along the sides. This dinosaur left its fossilized footprints in many parts of central and north-central Texas. The hind feet left huge saucerlike depressions with three claw marks up front. The front-foot tracks are smaller and resemble horseshoes. Scientists think that *Pleurocoelus* must have walked on the tips of its front toes which were enclosed in a kind of padded sheath.

TENONTOSAURUS

teh-non-toh-SORE-us

Tenontosaurus FACT BOX

Length: 20 feet
Weight: 1 ton
Time: 110 - 105 million years ago
Where Found: Texas, Oklahoma, Utah, Montana
Classification: An ornithopod, or a plant-eating bird-hip capable of standing on two legs.
Notable Notes: Bones of *Tenontosaurus* and teeth of *Deinonychus* are often found together. Maybe this means that packs of the much smaller *Deinonychus* sometimes attacked a *Tenontosaurus*.

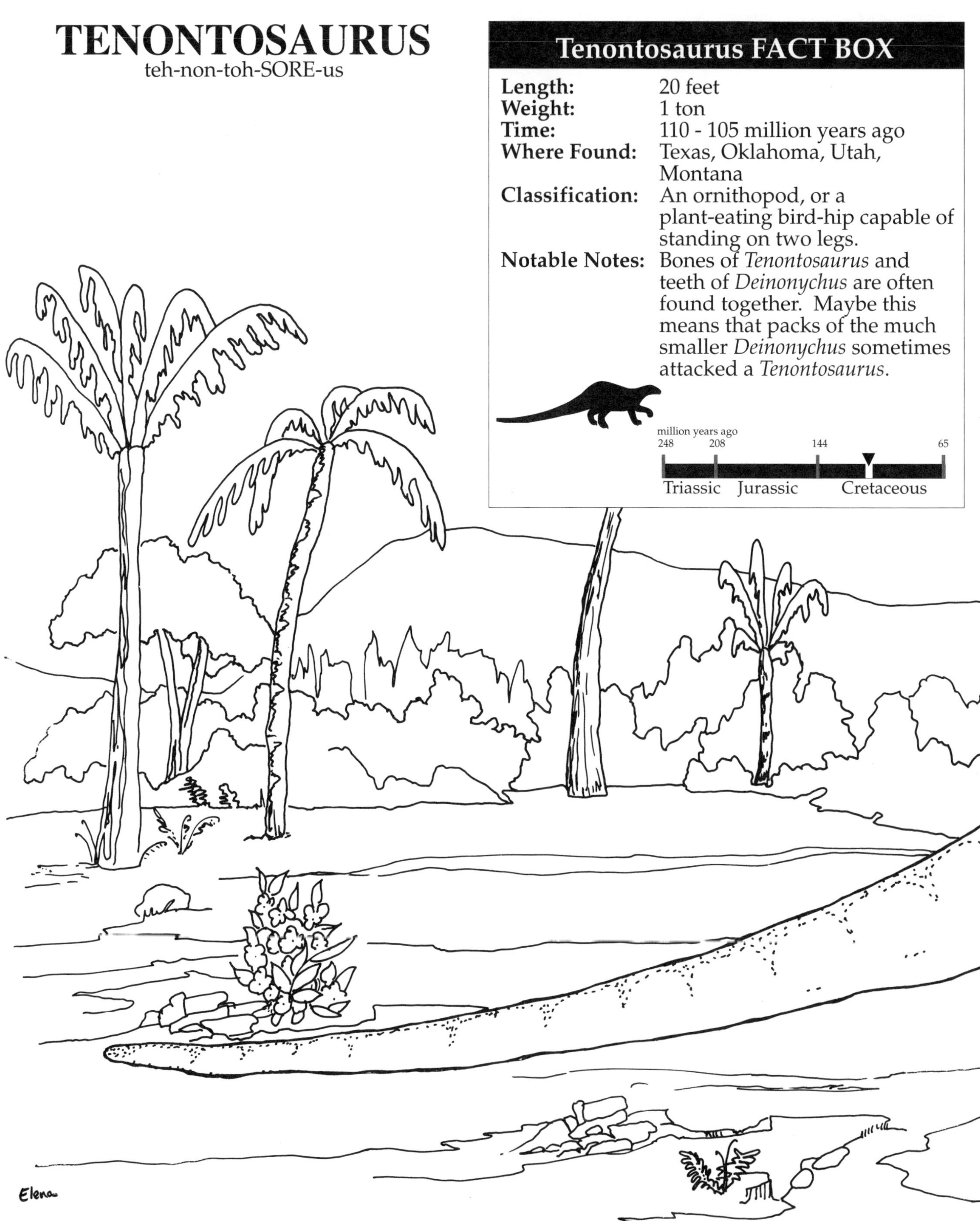

Tenontosaurus means "sinew lizard" from its powerful, sinewy tail. This dinosaur could walk on its hind legs, but went on all fours while feeding. Its very long, deep tail was probably used like a flail to keep attackers at bay.

IGUANODON

ig-WHA-noh-don

Iguanodon means "iguana tooth" because its teeth were similar to those of an iguana lizard, except much bigger. It could stand on its hind legs or walk on all-fours. The three toes on each hind foot ended in hoof-like claws, and each five-fingered forefoot had a spiked thumb for self defense. *Iguanodon* cropped vegetation with its horn-covered beak and roamed the land in herds.

Putting muscles and skin on Iguanodon

We can add muscles to the skeleton of *Iguanodon* by studying the shape of bone surfaces and the marks left by muscle attachments when this dinosaur was alive. After figuring out the muscles, we can wrap skin around the dinosaur and get a picture of what *Iguanodon* looked like. The final color can only be guessed at.

BATCH THREE

The largest and most recent "batch" of Texas dinosaurs comes from about 75 to 65 million years ago. Fossils of dinosaurs of that time are found in Late Cretaceous rocks located in the Big Bend region of Texas. During those days, that area was located directly to the west of a vast inland sea that cut across North America from the Gulf of Mexico to Alaska. The dinosaur bones were buried in deposits

laid down at the mouths of rivers flowing into this sea. Late Cretaceous dinosaurs lived in a world of flowering bushes and trees not too different from modern times. Among familiar trees were oaks, figs and magnolias. Animals living alongside these dinosaurs included the largest-ever pterosaur, *Quetzalcoatlus*, and a 60-foot-long giant crocodile called *Phobosuchus*.

ALAMOSAURUS
AL-a-moh-SORE-us

Alamosaurus FACT BOX

Length: 70 feet
Weight: 30 tons
Time: 75 - 65 million years ago
Where Found: Texas, New Mexico, Utah, Montana
Classification: A sauropod, or giant four-legged plant-eating lizard-hip.
Notable Notes: One of the few sauropods to be still around by Late Cretaceous times. Most had died out much earlier.

Alamosaurus means "Alamo lizard" after the famous mission defended by Texans against a Mexican army. This dinosaur had a relatively slender build. Its peg-shaped teeth were not suitable for chewing. Instead, plant food was swallowed whole and later broken down in the stomach.

TYRANNOSAURUS

tie-RAN-oh-SORE-us

Tyrannosaurus FACT BOX

Length:	39 feet
Weight:	6.5 tons
Time:	75 - 65 million years ago
Where Found:	Western Canada, western U.S. including Texas.
Classification:	A carnosaur or giant, two-legged meat-eating lizard-hip.
Notable Notes:	Several species of *Tyrannosaurus* are known. *Tyrannosaurus rex* is the best known of those species.

million years ago

248 208 144 65

Triassic Jurassic Cretaceous

Tyrannosaurus means "tyrant lizard" from its impressive size and appearance. This dinosaur probably traveled alone or in pairs to hunt down weak individuals among herds of duck-billed or horned dinosaurs. Carrion (dead meat) was also eaten. The huge 4-foot-long head, with 6-inch-high steak-knife teeth, was the main weapon of attack, while the tiny yet powerful forearms served as grappling hooks.

CHASMOSAURUS

kas-moh-SORE-us

Chasmosaurus FACT BOX

Length: 17 feet
Weight: 2.2 tons
Time: 75 - 65 million years ago
Where Found: Alberta, Canada; Texas
Classification: A ceratopsian or horned bird-hip.
Notable Notes: Males and females have slightly different neck frills. In life, the bony horn cores were covered with a horny sheath.

Chasmosaurus means "chasm lizard" from the wide openings in the bony neck frill. (These openings were covered with skin). This dinosaur, like all horned dinosaurs, traveled in herds and cropped low vegetation with its toothless beak. Behind the beak were teeth that meshed together like scissor-blades to slice up the cropped food. Rival males fought each other with their horns.

EDMONTOSAURUS

ed-MON-toh-SORE-us

Edmontosaurus FACT BOX

Length:	43 feet
Weight:	4 tons
Time:	75 - 65 million years ago
Where Found:	Much of western North America, including Texas
Classification:	A hadrosaur or duck-billed bird-hip.
Notable Notes:	Loose skin around the nose area could be blown up like a balloon to make a loud bellowing sound.

million years ago
248 208 144 65
Triassic Jurassic Cretaceous

Edmontosaurus means "Edmonton lizard" after the place in Canada where it was first found. This dinosaur stood or ambled on all fours but when moving quickly, sprinted on its hind legs. Herds of these peaceful vegetarians lived along the western shores of the great inland sea that covered North America during Late Cretaceous times.

PANOPLOSAURUS

PAN-oh-pluh-SORE-us

Panoplosaurus FACT BOX

Length: 23 feet
Weight: 4 tons
Time: 75 - 65 million years ago
Where Found: Alberta, Canada; Montana, Texas
Classification: An ankylosaur or armored bird-hip.
Notable Notes: The shape of the skull indicates that this dinosaur had large cheek pouches for food storage.

Panoplosaurus means "armored lizard" after the bony plates that covered its back and head. In addition, fierce-looking spines protected this four-legged dinosaur's shoulders and sides. Numerous ridged, leaf-shaped teeth sliced up juicy, low-growing vegetation picked off the ground.

TOROSAURUS

tor-roh-SORE-us

Torosaurus FACT BOX

Length:	24 feet
Weight:	9 tons
Time:	75 - 65 million years ago
Where Found:	Much of western North America, including Texas.
Classification:	A ceratopsian or horned bird-hip.
Notable Notes:	*Torosaurus* had the largest head of any known land animal. Its skull measured 9 feet in length, with the huge neck frill taking up half of that length.

million years ago
248 208 144 65
Triassic Jurassic Cretaceous

Torosaurus means "bull lizard" after the large cattle-like horns over the eyes. As in all horned dinosaurs, the neck frill provided attachment for some of the animal's powerful jaw muscles and it also protected the neck and the shoulder area.

KRITOSAURUS

KRI-toh-SORE-us

Kritosaurus FACT BOX

Length:	30 feet
Weight:	3 tons
Time:	75 - 65 million years ago
Where Found:	Alberta, Canada; Texas, New Mexico, Argentina
Classification:	A hadrosaur or duck-billed bird-hip.
Notable Notes:	Like all duckbills, food was cropped with a horny duck-like bill. Further back, the jaws were crammed with teeth arranged in plates for grinding up the food.

million years ago
248 208 144 65
Triassic Jurassic Cretaceous

Kritosaurus means "noble lizard" after its "Roman nose" shaped by the distinct bump over the snout. This dinosaur, like all duckbills, moved in herds, laid eggs in mud nests on the ground and guarded the hatched-out young.

ORNITHOMIMUS

OR-ni-thoh-MYE-mus

Ornithomimus FACT BOX

Length: 12 feet
Weight: 300 pounds
Time: 75 - 65 million years ago
Where Found: Western North America, including Texas
Classification: An ornithomimid or "ostrich" lizard-hip.
Notable Notes: A sharp-edged horny bill covered the toothless jaws. The top jaw could swing upward against the skull to provide a wide gape for handling large fruits or eggs.

million years ago
248 208 144 65
Triassic Jurassic Cretaceous

Ornithomimus means "bird-mimic" after its birdlike appearance. Long hind legs, a lightly-built skeleton and a stiff tail for counterbalance made this one of the fastest of the dinosaurs, capable of traveling up to 30 miles per hour.

STEGOCERAS

ste-GOS-er-us

Stegoceras FACT BOX

Length: 7 feet
Weight: 200 pounds
Time: 75 - 65 million years ago
Where Found: Alberta, Canada; Montana, Texas
Classification: A pachycephalosaur or bone-headed bird-hip.
Notable Notes: Males probably clashed their dome-like bony heads together at mating season like bighorn sheep do today.

million years ago
248 208 144 65
Triassic Jurassic Cretaceous

Stegoceras means "roof-horn" after its thick-domed skull, ringed with a fringe of small spikes. It ran on its hind legs with the back held level to the ground. Its diet consisted of soft plant materials along with insects.

Find the path through the dinosaur.

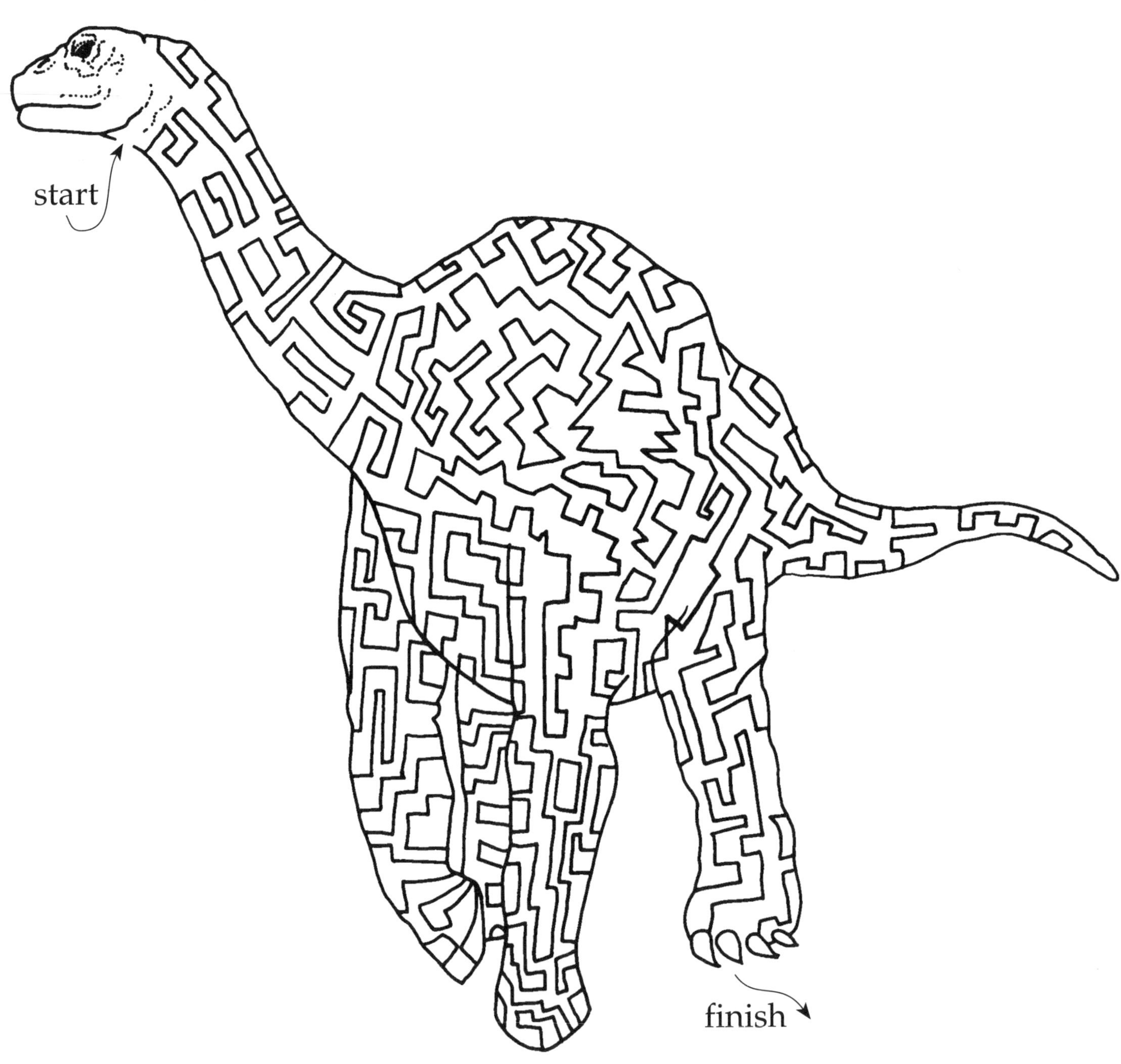

Lizard-hip or bird-hip?

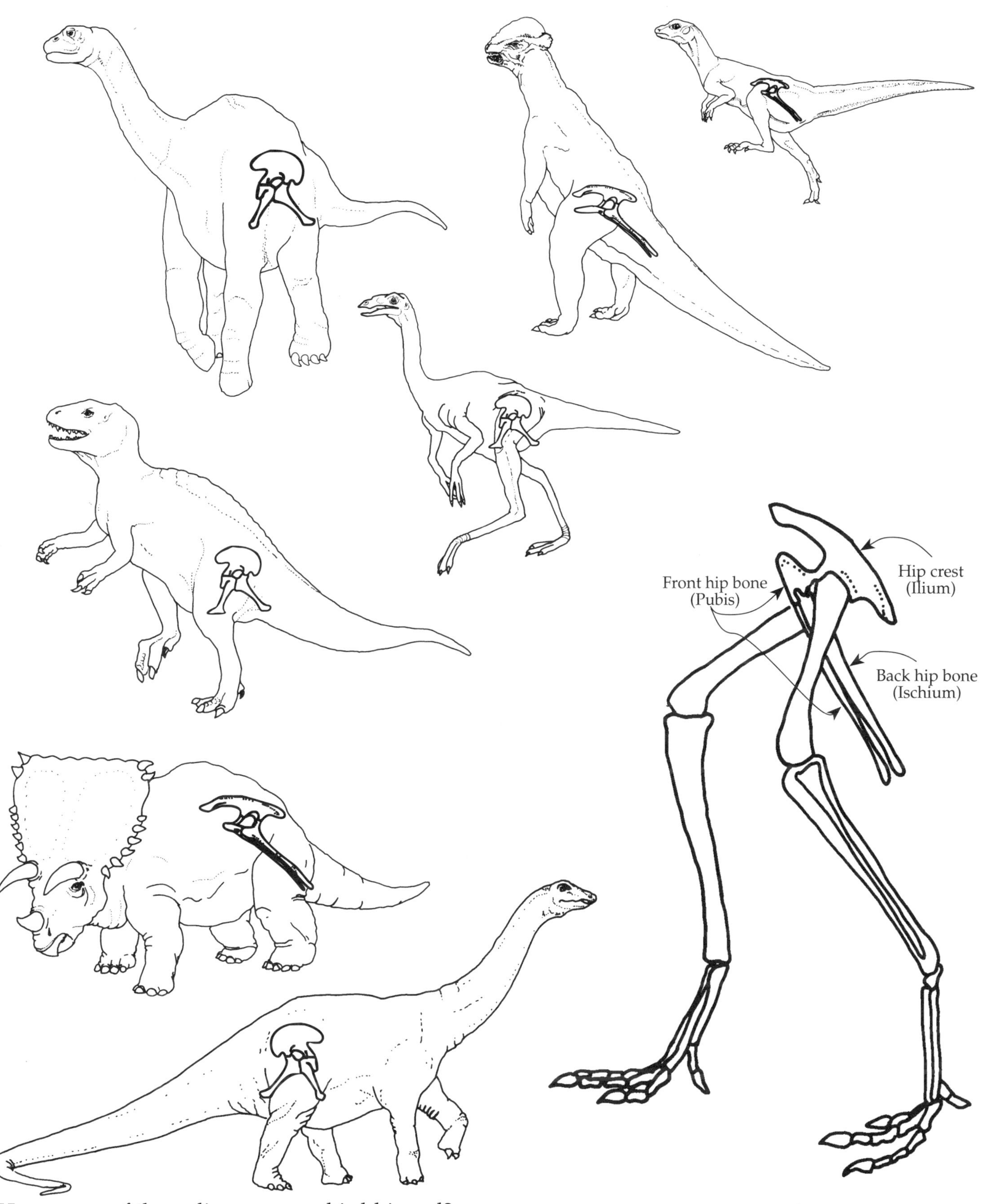

How many of these dinosaurs are bird-hipped?
How many of these dinosaurs are lizard-hipped?

Bird-hipped dinosaur hip bones and leg bones.

How dinosaurs get fossilized.

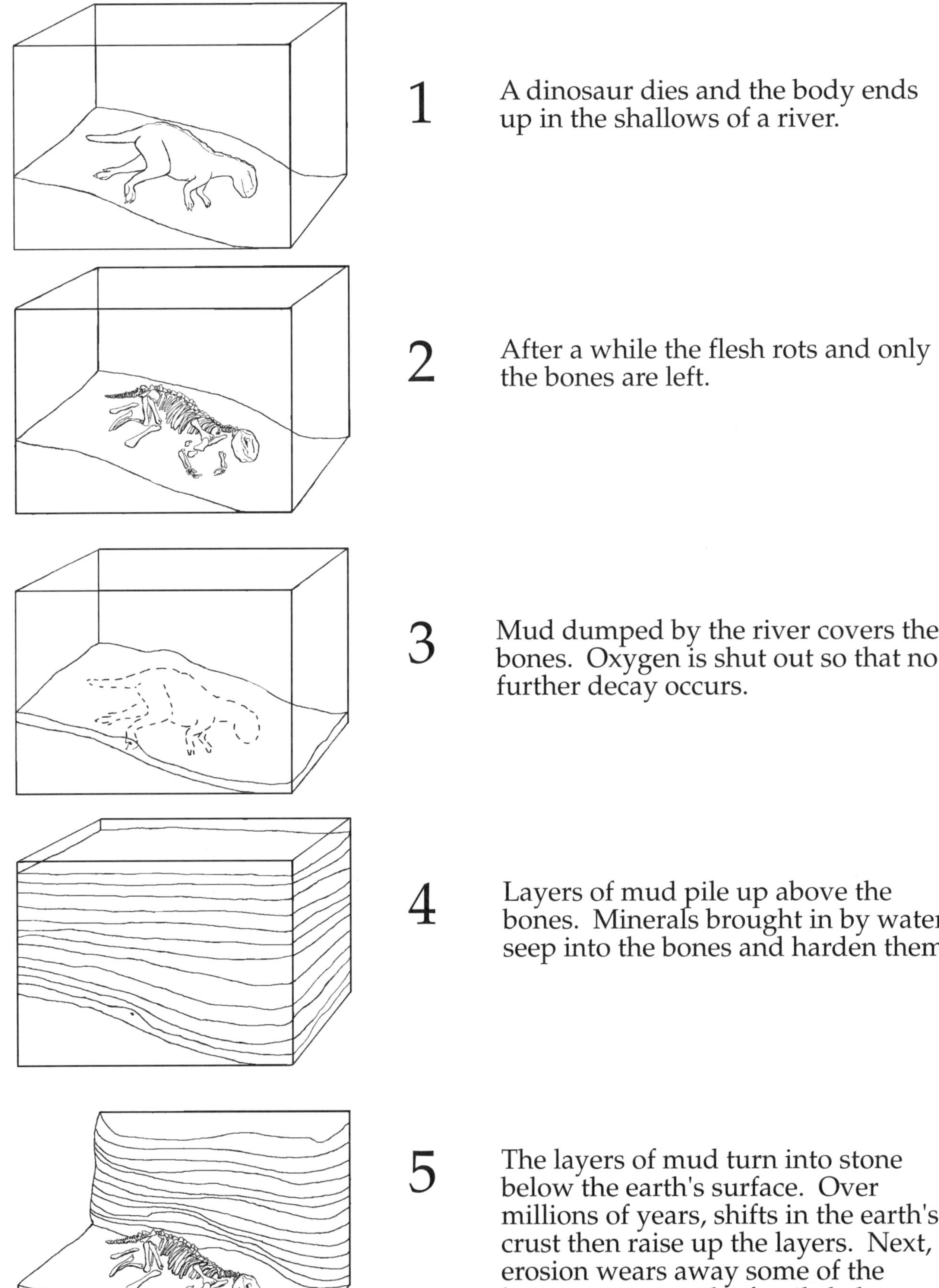

1 A dinosaur dies and the body ends up in the shallows of a river.

2 After a while the flesh rots and only the bones are left.

3 Mud dumped by the river covers the bones. Oxygen is shut out so that no further decay occurs.

4 Layers of mud pile up above the bones. Minerals brought in by water seep into the bones and harden them.

5 The layers of mud turn into stone below the earth's surface. Over millions of years, shifts in the earth's crust then raise up the layers. Next, erosion wears away some of the layers, exposing the fossil skeleton.

How to dig up a dinosaur.

Most often, fossil dinosaur skeletons are found still buried with only some of the bones showing at a road cut or the side of a cliff. Once discovered, teams of experts use heavy equipment and special tools to uncover the bones and get them back to the laboratory.

Uncovering the find, safely.

The right tools are needed to remove the fossils from the site and return them to the laboratory without being damaged.

Protective gear

It is important to wear proper protective clothing while on a fossil dig. Gloves are needed when hammering and chiseling are done, and goggles protect the eyes from sharp splinters of rock. A hard hat is advisable if work is being done near cliffs.

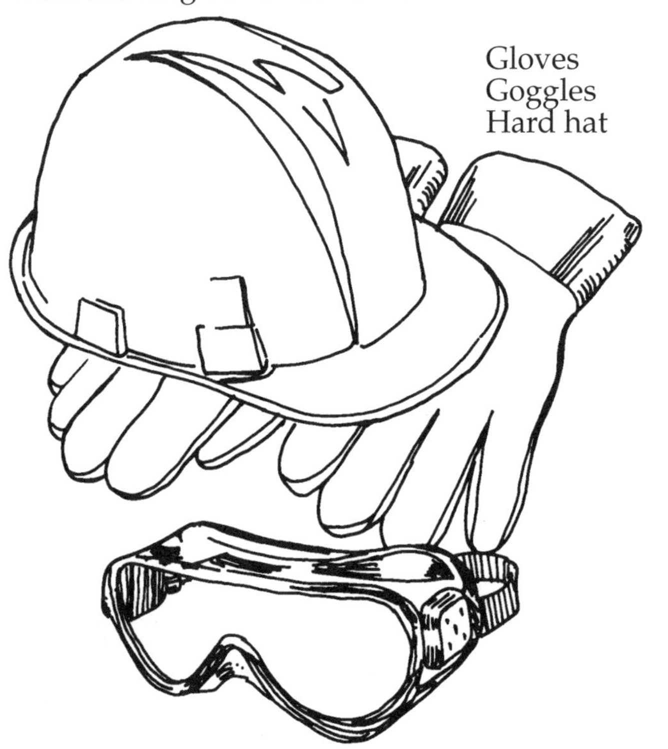

Uncovering a find

When the rock in which the fossils are embedded is very hard, a lump hammer is used to drive chisels into the rock. A wide variety of chisels can be used for getting into awkward corners.

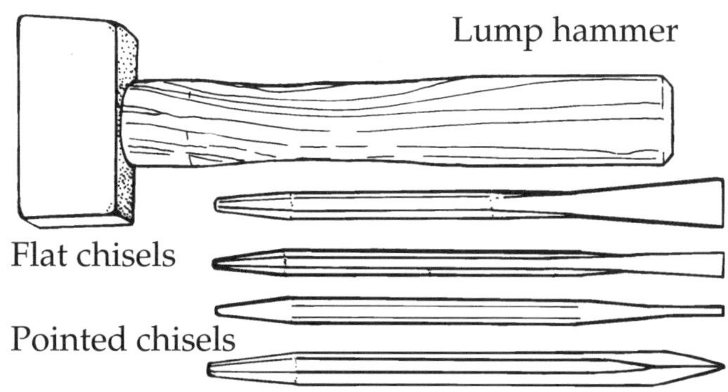

Paint brushes are used to clear away dust while the rock is being chipped away from the fossils. As a fossil is exposed, it is often painted with glue to secure any loose fragments.

Soft paint brush

Hard paint brush

Hammers and Saws

A variety of tools are used by paleontologists (fossil experts) in the field.

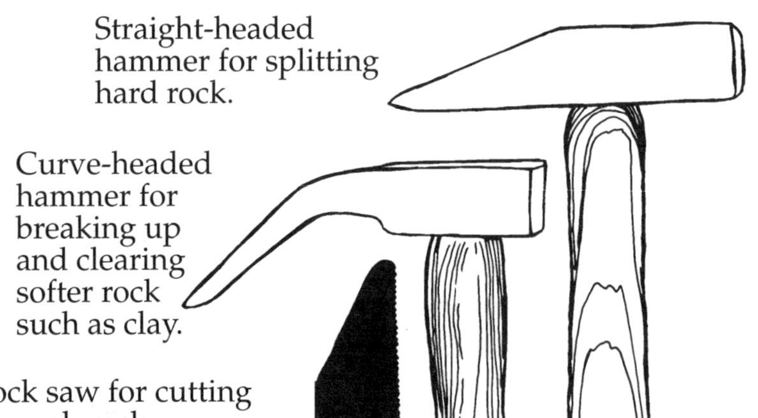

When fossils are exposed, they are sometimes encased in plaster jackets to protect them for transportation back to the laboratory.

To make a plaster jacket, the plaster is mixed with water to make a paste, then burlap or any open-weave fabric is dipped into the paste. The rock and fossil are covered with a layer of wet tissue paper before the plaster is applied. This keeps the plaster from sticking to the rock and fossil.

How to dress a dinosaur bone.

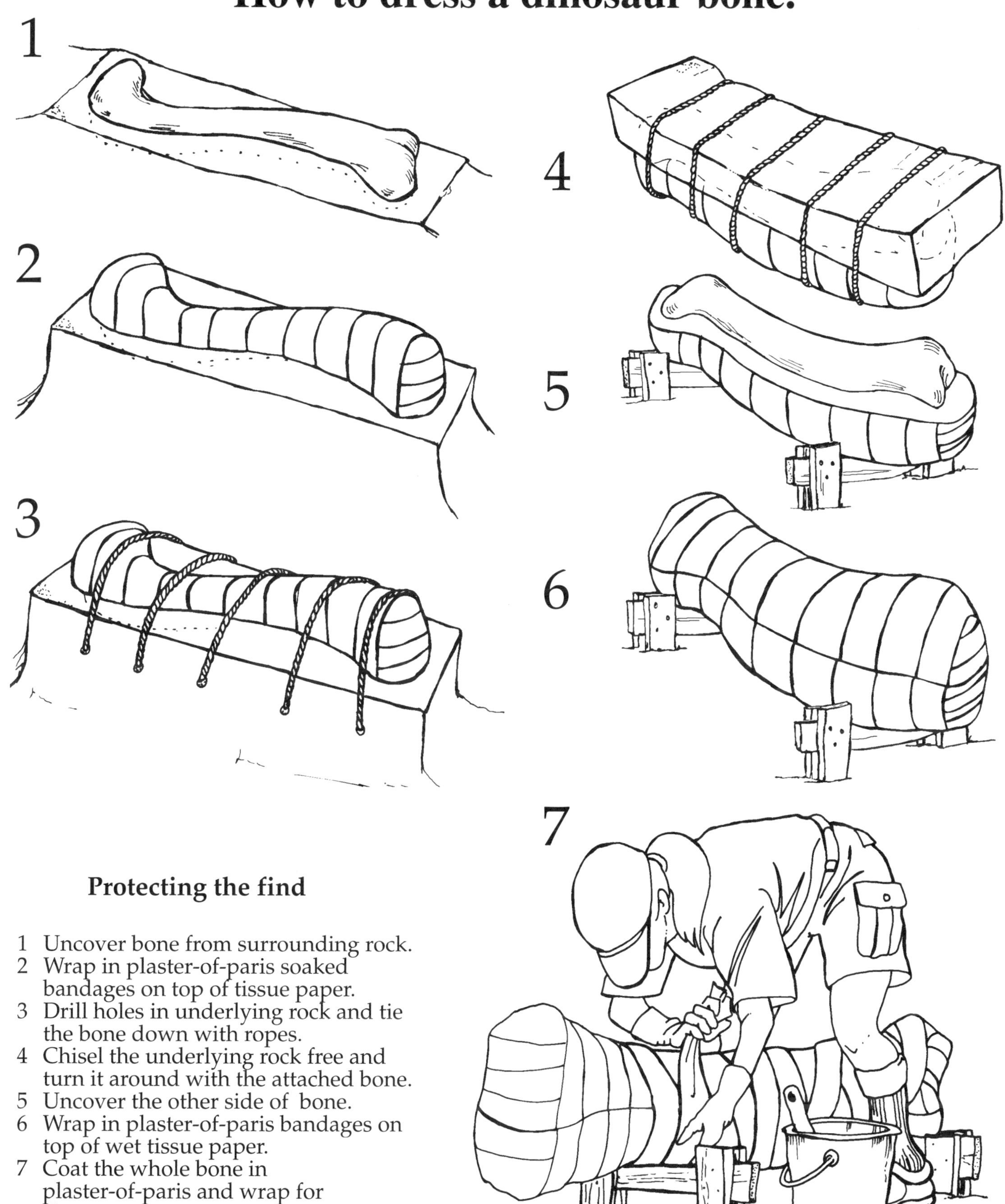

Protecting the find

1 Uncover bone from surrounding rock.
2 Wrap in plaster-of-paris soaked bandages on top of tissue paper.
3 Drill holes in underlying rock and tie the bone down with ropes.
4 Chisel the underlying rock free and turn it around with the attached bone.
5 Uncover the other side of bone.
6 Wrap in plaster-of-paris bandages on top of wet tissue paper.
7 Coat the whole bone in plaster-of-paris and wrap for shipment.

Which are the two identical sets of Technosaurus?

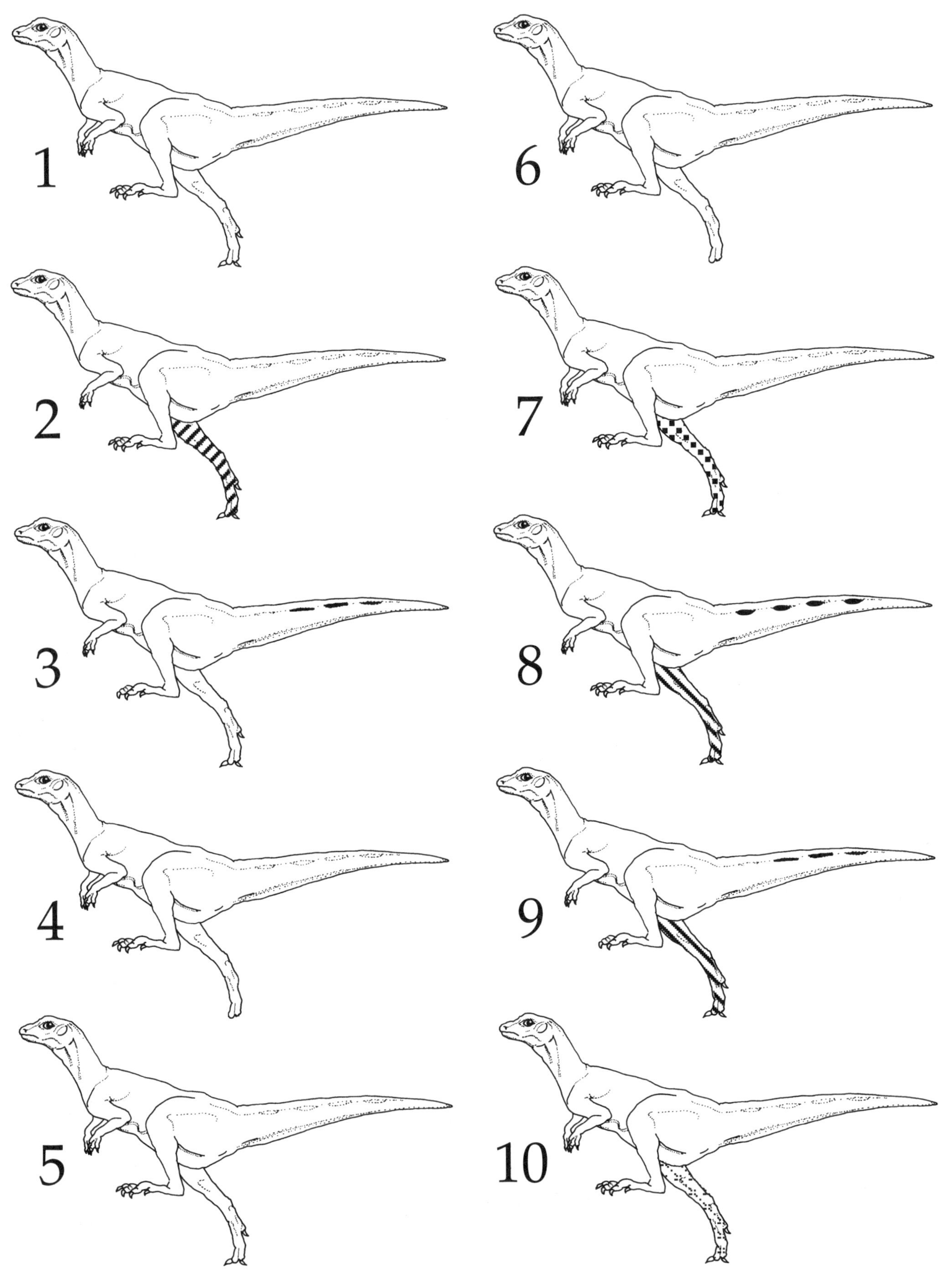

1 and 5, 4 and 6

Find the path through the passages to the fossils.

EDMONTOSAURUS
and family

Some duckbilled dinosaurs built nests with raised mud rims.
How many eggs did this Edmontosaurus lay?

twenty

Word Search Game

ACROCANTHOSAURUS
ALAMOSAURUS
ARCHEOLOGY
ARMOR-PLATED
BEDROCK
BONE
CARNIVORE
CLAY
COLD-BLOODED
CRETACEOUS
DINOSAURS
ERA
FORMATION
FOSSIL
GENERA
GEOLOGY
JURASSIC
LIMESTONE
LIZARDS
PALEONTOLOGY
PLEUROCOELUS
PREHISTORIC
QUETZALCOATLUS
READING
SAUROPOD
TEETH
TEXAS
TRIASSIC
TURTLE
TYRANNOSAURUS

A	C	R	O	C	A	N	T	H	O	S	A	U	R	U	S	P
	R	E	A	D	I	N	G		A					U		R
T	E	E					T	U	R	T	L	E	L			E
Y	T						R					T	E	E	T	H
R	A			G	F	O	S	S	I	L	A					I
A	C			E	P					O						S
N	E			O					C	I	S	S	A	I	R	T
N	O		D	L				L	I	Z	A	R	D	S		O
O	U	E	N	O	B	C	A	R	N	I	V	O	R	E		R
S	S			G		Z						D				I
A				Y	T					A	E					C
U	Y	A	R	E	N	E	G		R	D					S	
R	G		U					M	O					C	U	
U	O	Q					O	O					I		L	
S	L					R	L					S			E	Y
	O				P	B					S				O	G
	T			L	D	I	N	O	S	A	U	R	S		C	O
	N		A	L	I				R						O	L
	O	T	O		N			U							R	O
	E	C			O		J	B	E	D	R	O	C	K	U	E
D	L				S		L	I	M	E	S	T	O	N	E	H
	A				A								Y	A	L	C
	P				U	N	O	I	T	A	M	R	O	F	P	R
T	E	X	A	S	R	S	U	R	U	A	S	O	M	A	L	A

Find the path through the dinosaur.

Find the path through the passages to the fossils.

The information contained in this book is based on research published by many distinguished vertebrate paleontologists. Special thanks, however, are due to:

DR. WANN LANGSTON
Vertebrate Paleontology Laboratory
University of Texas at Austin
Austin, Texas

DR. JAMES O. FARLOW
Department of Geosciences
Indiana University-Purdue University
Fort Wayne, Indiana

DR. SANKAR CHATTERJEE
Museum of Texas Tech University
Lubbock, Texas